Delicious Carnivore Slow Cooker Recipes For Tender Meals

Easy Meat Dishes With Vibrant Photos And Clear Steps

By Diana Stone

Copyright © by Diana Stone

Disclaimer:

Introduction

Welcome to Delicious Carnivore Slow Cooker Recipes For Tender Meals, where flavorful, satisfying dishes come to life with ease. Whether you're a carnivore diet enthusiast or simply looking for easy-to-make, hearty meals, this cookbook will become your trusted kitchen companion.

If you're ready to explore tender, slow-cooked meals that are full of flavor and health benefits, you've come to the right place. This cookbook is designed to cater to those who follow the carnivore diet but also to anyone seeking delicious, protein-packed meals.

This book features 50 carefully crafted recipes, divided into 5 distinct chapters:

- ✓ **Meat**
- ✓ **Chicken**
- ✓ **Fish**
- ✓ **Seafood**
- ✓ **Soup**

Each chapter offers 10 unique and delicious recipes that are not only carnivore-friendly but also tailored to promote balanced blood sugar levels. With original and colorful photographs accompanying every recipe, you'll have visual guidance and motivation to try every dish.

What sets this cookbook apart is its simplicity. Every recipe is easy to follow, featuring step-by-step instructions and requiring minimal ingredients. This ensures that anyone, regardless of cooking experience, can successfully prepare mouthwatering meals. Plus, each recipe has been tested for perfect results every time, promising flawless flavors. All recipes are presented in vibrant color, making the book a joy to use and visually appealing.

Dive into this cookbook to enjoy the benefits of:

- ✓ Authentic, original recipes
- ✓ Colorful, vibrant photos for each dish
- ✓ Standard color printing for paperback
- ✓ Easy-to-follow instructions
- ✓ Get ready to savor meals that support your health goals without sacrificing flavor.

Let's begin your journey toward tasty, balanced living with Delicious Carnivore Slow Cooker Recipes For Tender Meals by Diana Stone!

Table of Contents

Chapter 01: Savory Meats

Recipe 01: Slow Cooked Goat Curry

Enjoy a hearty and flavorful dish with this slow-cooked goat curry, perfectly paired with tender potatoes and carrots. The rich, meaty flavors are enhanced with a sprinkle of fresh parsley, offering a satisfying meal that's easy to prepare using your slow cooker.

Servings: 4

Prepping Time: 15 minutes

Cook Time: 6 hours

Difficulty: Easy

Ingredients:

- ✓ 1 lb goat meat, cubed
- ✓ 2 large potatoes, chopped
- ✓ 3 medium carrots, chopped
- ✓ 1 large onion, diced
- ✓ 4 garlic cloves, minced
- ✓ 1 tsp paprika
- ✓ 1 tsp ground cumin
- ✓ 1 tsp black pepper
- ✓ 1 cup beef broth
- ✓ Salt to taste
- ✓ Fresh parsley, chopped (for garnish)

Step-by-Step Preparation:

1. In a slow cooker, combine goat meat, potatoes, carrots, onion, and garlic.
2. Sprinkle paprika, cumin, black pepper, and salt over the ingredients.
3. Pour in beef broth and stir to mix everything well.
4. Set your slow cooker on low and cook for 6 hours until the meat is tender.
5. Serve with freshly chopped parsley on top.

Nutritional Facts: (Per serving):

- ❖ Calories: 350
- ❖ Protein: 30g
- ❖ Fat: 18g
- ❖ Carbohydrates: 20g
- ❖ Fiber: 4g

This carnivore-friendly slow-cooked goat curry is an ideal meal for a hearty dinner. Packed with rich flavors and tender meat, this dish is sure to become a favorite in your meal rotation. Enjoy the simplicity and deliciousness of this wholesome recipe!

Recipe 02: Slow Cooker Thick and Chunky Beef Stew

This hearty, thick, and chunky beef stew is the perfect comfort food for a carnivore diet. Slow-cooked to perfection, this rich, meaty stew will keep you satisfied and energized. Packed with tender chunks of beef and bold flavors, it's a simple, nourishing meal that's easy to prepare in a slow cooker.

Servings: 4

Prepping Time: 10 minutes

Cook Time: 6-8 hours

Difficulty: Easy

Ingredients:

- ✓ 2 lbs beef chuck roast, cut into chunks
- ✓ 1 large onion, diced
- ✓ 4 garlic cloves, minced
- ✓ 2 cups beef broth
- ✓ 1 tsp sea salt
- ✓ 1 tsp black pepper
- ✓ 1 tsp thyme
- ✓ 2 bay leaves
- ✓ Fresh parsley for garnish (optional)

Step-by-Step Preparation:

1. Place beef chunks, onion, and garlic in the slow cooker.
2. Season with sea salt, black pepper, and thyme.
3. Pour beef broth over the ingredients and add the bay leaves.
4. Cover and cook on low for 6-8 hours until the beef is tender.
5. Remove bay leaves and serve with fresh parsley on top, if desired.

Nutritional Facts: (Per serving):

- ❖ Calories: 450
- ❖ Protein: 40g
- ❖ Fat: 30g
- ❖ Carbohydrates: 4g
- ❖ Fiber: 0g

This thick and chunky beef stew is a perfect dish for anyone following a carnivore diet. It's flavorful, easy to prepare, and full of hearty, nutrient-dense meat that will leave you feeling satisfied and nourished. Enjoy the rich taste of slow-cooked beef in every bite!

Recipe 03: Meat Stew With Vegetables in Tomato Sauce

This flavorful meat stew with vegetables in tomato sauce is a carnivore diet delight. Slow-cooked to tender perfection, this hearty dish combines rich beef with a savory tomato sauce and vegetables for a satisfying, nutrient-packed meal that's easy to prepare in your slow cooker.

Servings: 4

Prepping Time: 15 minutes

Cook Time: 6-7 hours

Difficulty: Easy

Ingredients:

- ✓ 2 lbs beef stew meat, cubed
- ✓ 2 carrots, chopped
- ✓ 1 large onion, diced
- ✓ 2 cloves garlic, minced
- ✓ 1 cup beef broth
- ✓ 1 can (15 oz) crushed tomatoes
- ✓ 1 tsp salt
- ✓ 1 tsp black pepper
- ✓ 1 tsp oregano
- ✓ 2 bay leaves

Step-by-Step Preparation:

1. Place beef stew meat, carrots, onion, and garlic in the slow cooker.
2. Add salt, black pepper, and oregano to the mixture.
3. Pour in the beef broth and crushed tomatoes, then stir to combine.
4. Add the bay leaves on top and cover the slow cooker.
5. Cook on low for 6-7 hours until the meat is tender.
6. Remove bay leaves and serve hot.

Nutritional Facts: (Per serving):

- ❖ Calories: 400
- ❖ Protein: 35g
- ❖ Fat: 22g
- ❖ Carbohydrates: 10g
- ❖ Fiber: 3g

Enjoy this savory, rich meat stew that fits perfectly into a carnivore diet. The tender beef combined with a flavorful tomato sauce and vegetables offers a wholesome, delicious meal that's perfect for any occasion. Simple to prepare and packed with nutrients, this dish will be a favorite!

Recipe 04: Meat Stew With Potato, Carrot and Green Pea

This hearty meat stew, slow-cooked with potatoes, carrots, and green peas in a rich tomato sauce, is a perfect carnivore-friendly meal. Packed with flavor and tender ingredients, this dish offers a satisfying, nutrient-dense option for any mealtime, all made effortlessly in a slow cooker.

Servings: 4

Prepping Time: 15 minutes

Cook Time: 6-7 hours

Difficulty: Easy

Ingredients:

- ✓ 2 lbs beef stew meat, cubed
- ✓ 2 large potatoes, diced
- ✓ 2 carrots, chopped
- ✓ 1 cup green peas
- ✓ 1 large onion, diced
- ✓ 2 garlic cloves, minced
- ✓ 1 can (15 oz) crushed tomatoes
- ✓ 1 cup beef broth
- ✓ 1 tsp salt
- ✓ 1 tsp black pepper
- ✓ 1 tsp paprika
- ✓ 2 bay leaves

Step-by-Step Preparation:

1. Add beef, potatoes, carrots, green peas, onion, and garlic to the slow cooker.
2. Season with salt, black pepper, and paprika.
3. Pour in crushed tomatoes and beef broth, stirring to combine.
4. Place bay leaves on top and cover.
5. Cook on low for 6-7 hours, or until meat and vegetables are tender.
6. Remove bay leaves and serve hot.

Nutritional Facts: (Per serving):

- ❖ Calories: 420
- ❖ Protein: 35g
- ❖ Fat: 18g
- ❖ Carbohydrates: 28g
- ❖ Fiber: 5g

Enjoy this hearty and flavorful meat stew, a perfect slow cooker recipe for carnivore diet enthusiasts. Packed with tender meat and a rich, savory tomato sauce, it's a wholesome, filling meal that's simple to prepare and bursting with comfort food goodness. Ideal for busy days or cozy nights!

Recipe 05: Beef and Vegetable Casserole

This delicious beef and vegetable casserole, slow-cooked to perfection and served with rice, is a hearty meal designed for carnivore diet lovers. Packed with tender beef and nutrient-rich vegetables, this dish is simple to prepare and ideal for satisfying your hunger with wholesome, comforting flavors.

Servings: 4

Prepping Time: 15 minutes

Cook Time: 6-7 hours

Difficulty: Easy

Ingredients:

✓ 2 lbs beef stew meat, cubed

✓ 1 large carrot, chopped

✓ 1 large zucchini, sliced

✓ 1 bell pepper, diced

✓ 1 large onion, diced

✓ 2 garlic cloves, minced

✓ 1 can (15 oz) diced tomatoes

✓ 1 cup beef broth

✓ 1 tsp salt

✓ 1 tsp black pepper

✓ 1 tsp thyme

✓ 1 cup cooked rice (for serving)

Step-by-Step Preparation:

1. Place beef, carrot, zucchini, bell pepper, onion, and garlic in the slow cooker.

2. Season with salt, black pepper, and thyme.

3. Pour diced tomatoes and beef broth over the ingredients, stirring to combine.

4. Cover and cook on low for 6-7 hours until the beef is tender.

5. Serve the casserole hot over a bed of cooked rice.

Nutritional Facts: (Per serving):

❖ Calories: 480

❖ Protein: 35g

❖ Fat: 22g

❖ Carbohydrates: 35g

❖ Fiber: 5g

This beef and vegetable casserole, served with rice, offers a perfect balance of rich, tender beef and healthy vegetables. The slow-cooked flavors make it a comforting, satisfying meal that's easy to prepare and enjoy any day of the week. Dig in for a filling, nutritious meal packed with flavor!

Recipe 06: Boeuf Bourguignon With Boletus Edulis Mushrooms

This rich and flavorful Boeuf Bourguignon with Boletus Edulis mushrooms is a luxurious carnivore-friendly dish. Slow-cooked to perfection, this French classic combines tender beef with the earthy, gourmet flavor of Boletus mushrooms, offering a satisfying and elegant meal that's easy to prepare in your slow cooker.

Servings: 4

Prepping Time: 20 minutes

Cook Time: 6-8 hours

Difficulty: Medium

Ingredients:

- 2 lbs beef chuck, cubed
- 1 cup Boletus Edulis mushrooms (or porcini), sliced
- 1 large onion, diced
- 4 garlic cloves, minced
- 1 cup red wine
- 1 cup beef broth
- 2 tbsp tomato paste
- 1 tsp thyme
- 2 bay leaves
- 1 tsp salt
- 1 tsp black pepper
- 1 tbsp butter (for browning)

Step-by-Step Preparation:

1. In a skillet, heat butter and brown the beef cubes on all sides. Transfer to the slow cooker.
2. In the same skillet, sauté onions, garlic, and Boletus Edulis mushrooms until fragrant.
3. Add the sautéed vegetables to the slow cooker along with tomato paste, red wine, and beef broth.
4. Season with thyme, salt, and black pepper, and add bay leaves.
5. Cook on low for 6-8 hours until the beef is tender.
6. Remove bay leaves before serving.

Nutritional Facts: (Per serving):

- Calories: 520
- Protein: 45g
- Fat: 30g
- Carbohydrates: 8g
- Fiber: 2g

This Boeuf Bourguignon with Boletus Edulis mushrooms is a gourmet carnivore recipe that delivers both flavor and satisfaction. The slow cooking brings out the tender richness of the beef and the earthy depth of the mushrooms, making it a perfect choice for a special, nourishing m

Recipe 07: Chicken Stew With Potatoes and Vegetables

This hearty chicken stew with potatoes and vegetables is a perfect carnivore diet slow cooker recipe. Packed with tender chicken and flavorful vegetables, this dish is comforting and nutritious, offering a wholesome meal that's easy to prepare with minimal effort.

Servings: 4

Prepping Time: 15 minutes

Cook Time: 6-7 hours

Difficulty: Easy

Ingredients:

- ✓ 2 lbs chicken thighs, bone-in and skinless
- ✓ 3 large potatoes, diced
- ✓ 2 carrots, chopped
- ✓ 1 onion, diced
- ✓ 2 cloves garlic, minced
- ✓ 1 cup chicken broth
- ✓ 1 tsp salt
- ✓ 1 tsp black pepper
- ✓ 1 tsp thyme
- ✓ 1 bay leaf

Step-by-Step Preparation:

1. Place chicken thighs, potatoes, carrots, onion, and garlic into the slow cooker.

2. Season with salt, black pepper, and thyme.

3. Pour in the chicken broth and add the bay leaf.

4. Cover and cook on low for 6-7 hours, or until the chicken and vegetables are tender.

5. Remove the bay leaf before serving.

Nutritional Facts: (Per serving):

- ❖ Calories: 380
- ❖ Protein: 30g
- ❖ Fat: 18g
- ❖ Carbohydrates: 25g
- ❖ Fiber: 4g

Enjoy this flavorful and hearty chicken stew, perfect for carnivore diet enthusiasts. The slow-cooked chicken combined with tender vegetables offers a delicious and nourishing meal that's easy to prepare. A great option for a cozy, satisfying dinner!

Recipe 08: Pork Roast and Vegetables

This savory pork roast with vegetables is a hearty and satisfying carnivore-friendly dish. Slow-cooked to perfection, the pork becomes tender and juicy, while the vegetables soak up the rich flavors, creating a wholesome meal that's easy to prepare in your slow cooker.

Servings: 6

Prepping Time: 15 minutes

Cook Time: 6-8 hours

Difficulty: Easy

Ingredients:

- ✓ 3 lbs pork shoulder roast
- ✓ 3 large carrots, chopped
- ✓ 4 medium potatoes, diced
- ✓ 1 large onion, sliced
- ✓ 2 garlic cloves, minced

- ✓ 1 cup chicken broth
- ✓ 1 tsp salt
- ✓ 1 tsp black pepper
- ✓ 1 tsp rosemary
- ✓ 2 bay leaves

Step-by-Step Preparation:

1. Place pork roast in the slow cooker and arrange carrots, potatoes, onion, and garlic around it.
2. Season with salt, black pepper, and rosemary.
3. Pour chicken broth over the ingredients and add bay leaves.
4. Cover and cook on low for 6-8 hours until the pork is tender.
5. Remove bay leaves before serving.

Nutritional Facts: (Per serving):

- ❖ Calories: 450
- ❖ Protein: 35g
- ❖ Fat: 25g

- ❖ Carbohydrates: 18g
- ❖ Fiber: 4g

This pork roast and vegetables recipe is a perfect balance of tender meat and flavorful vegetables. Slow cooking allows the flavors to meld beautifully, making it a wholesome and satisfying meal for the carnivore diet. Enjoy a comforting, hearty dish that's simple yet delicious!

Recipe 09: Beef Brisket With Coleslaw and Thyme

This tender, slow-cooked beef brisket with coleslaw and a touch of thyme is a perfect carnivore diet meal. The rich flavors of the brisket, paired with the refreshing crunch of coleslaw, create a satisfying and hearty dish that's easy to prepare in your slow cooker.

Servings: 6

Prepping Time: 15 minutes

Cook Time: 8-10 hours

Difficulty: Easy

Ingredients:

- ✓ 3 lbs beef brisket
- ✓ 1 large onion, sliced
- ✓ 4 garlic cloves, minced
- ✓ 1 cup beef broth
- ✓ 2 tsp thyme
- ✓ 1 tsp salt
- ✓ 1 tsp black pepper

- ✓ 1/2 head of cabbage, shredded (for coleslaw)
- ✓ 1 carrot, grated (for coleslaw)
- ✓ 1/4 cup mayonnaise (for coleslaw)
- ✓ 1 tbsp apple cider vinegar (for coleslaw)
- ✓ Salt and pepper to taste (for coleslaw)

Step-by-Step Preparation:

1. Place the beef brisket in the slow cooker and top with onion, garlic, thyme, salt, and black pepper.
2. Pour beef broth over the brisket.
3. Cover and cook on low for 8-10 hours until the brisket is tender.
4. While the brisket cooks, mix cabbage, carrot, mayonnaise, and apple cider vinegar in a bowl for coleslaw. Season with salt and pepper.
5. Serve the brisket hot with the coleslaw on the side.

Nutritional Facts: (Per serving):

- ❖ Calories: 520
- ❖ Protein: 45g
- ❖ Fat: 35g

- ❖ Carbohydrates: 8g
- ❖ Fiber: 2g

This beef brisket with coleslaw and thyme is a flavorful and wholesome meal for carnivore diet followers. The slow-cooked brisket is tender and juicy, complemented by the crisp and refreshing coleslaw. Simple to prepare and packed with flavor, it's the perfect meal for any occasion!

Recipe 10: Thai Beef Massaman Curry

This Thai Beef Massaman Curry is a rich, aromatic carnivore dish that's slow-cooked to perfection. The combination of tender beef and bold spices creates a flavorful, satisfying meal that's easy to prepare in your slow cooker. It's a delightful fusion of classic Thai flavors tailored for the carnivore diet.

Servings: 4

Prepping Time: 20 minutes

Cook Time: 6-8 hours

Difficulty: Medium

Ingredients:

- ✓ 2 lbs beef chuck, cubed
- ✓ 1 onion, diced
- ✓ 4 garlic cloves, minced
- ✓ 1 cup coconut milk
- ✓ 1 cup beef broth
- ✓ 2 tbsp Massaman curry paste
- ✓ 2 tbsp fish sauce
- ✓ 1 tbsp tamarind paste
- ✓ 1 tsp ground cinnamon
- ✓ 2 bay leaves
- ✓ 1 tsp salt
- ✓ 1 tsp black pepper

Step-by-Step Preparation:

1. Place the beef, onion, and garlic in the slow cooker.
2. In a bowl, mix coconut milk, beef broth, Massaman curry paste, fish sauce, tamarind paste, cinnamon, salt, and pepper. Pour the mixture over the beef.
3. Add bay leaves on top.
4. Cover and cook on low for 6-8 hours, or until the beef is tender.
5. Remove the bay leaves before serving.

Nutritional Facts: (Per serving):

- ❖ Calories: 480
- ❖ Protein: 38g
- ❖ Fat: 30g
- ❖ Carbohydrates: 10g
- ❖ Fiber: 2g

This Thai Beef Massaman Curry is a perfect carnivore-friendly dish that brings together rich, bold flavors with tender, slow-cooked beef. The aromatic spices and coconut milk make this a comforting and satisfying meal, ideal for a cozy night or to impress your dinner guests!

Chapter 02: Tender Chicken

Recipe 11: Slow Cooker Chicken Cacciatore

Slow Cooker Chicken Cacciatore is a delicious and hearty dish, perfect for a flavorful, comforting meal. This carnivore-friendly recipe brings together tender chicken, juicy tomatoes, bell peppers, carrots, and mushrooms, all slow-cooked to perfection.

Servings: 4

Prepping Time: 15 minutes

Cook Time: 6 hours

Difficulty: Easy

Ingredients:

- ✓ 4 chicken thighs, skin on
- ✓ 1 can (14 oz) diced tomatoes
- ✓ 2 bell peppers, sliced
- ✓ 2 carrots, chopped
- ✓ 1 cup mushrooms, sliced
- ✓ 1 onion, sliced
- ✓ 3 garlic cloves, minced
- ✓ 1 tsp dried oregano
- ✓ Salt and pepper to taste

Step-by-Step Preparation:

1. In a slow cooker, layer the chicken thighs at the bottom.
2. Add the sliced onions, bell peppers, carrots, and mushrooms on top.
3. Pour in the diced tomatoes and garlic, ensuring everything is coated.
4. Sprinkle oregano, salt, and pepper over the mixture.
5. Cover and cook on low for 6 hours until the chicken is tender.
6. Serve hot, and enjoy your flavorful meal.

Nutritional Facts: (Per serving)

- ❖ Calories: 320
- ❖ Protein: 30g
- ❖ Fat: 18g
- ❖ Carbohydrates: 10g
- ❖ Fiber: 3g

This Slow Cooker Chicken Cacciatore is not only a wholesome carnivore dish but also a great way to enjoy nutrient-packed vegetables. Easy to prepare and bursting with flavor, it's the perfect recipe to keep you satisfied and energized throughout the day.

Recipe 12: Shredded Chicken in Cream Cheese Sauce and Bacon

Indulge in the richness of this carnivore-friendly Shredded Chicken in Cream Cheese Sauce with crispy bacon. This easy slow cooker recipe creates a creamy, flavorful dish that melts in your mouth, making it a perfect comfort meal packed with protein and satisfying fats.

Servings: 4

Prepping Time: 10 minutes

Cook Time: 6 hours

Difficulty: Easy

Ingredients:

- ✓ 4 boneless, skinless chicken breasts
- ✓ 8 oz cream cheese, softened
- ✓ 6 slices of bacon, cooked and crumbled
- ✓ 1/2 cup chicken broth
- ✓ 1 tsp garlic powder
- ✓ Salt and pepper to taste

Step-by-Step Preparation:

1. Place chicken breasts in the slow cooker and season with garlic powder, salt, and pepper.

2. Add the softened cream cheese and chicken broth over the chicken.

3. Cover and cook on low for 6 hours until the chicken is tender.

4. Shred the chicken using two forks and mix it with the creamy sauce.

5. Stir in the crumbled bacon and serve hot.

Nutritional Facts: (Per serving)

- ✓ Calories: 400
- ✓ Protein: 32g
- ✓ Fat: 28g
- ✓ Carbohydrates: 3g

This Shredded Chicken in Cream Cheese Sauce and Bacon is a rich, savory dish that delivers comforting flavors in every bite. Easy to prepare, it's the perfect choice for anyone following the carnivore diet and looking for a delicious, satisfying meal.

Recipe 13: Slow Cooker Chicken Drumsticks

Slow Cooker Chicken Drumsticks are a simple yet delicious carnivore diet recipe. With just a few ingredients and slow cooking, you'll enjoy tender, juicy drumsticks packed with flavor. This recipe is perfect for a hassle-free meal that's full of protein and healthy fats.

Servings: 4   **Cook Time:** 6 hours

Prepping Time: 10 minutes   **Difficulty:** Easy

Ingredients:

- ✓ 8 chicken drumsticks
- ✓ 1/2 cup chicken broth
- ✓ 2 tbsp butter
- ✓ 1 tsp garlic powder
- ✓ 1 tsp smoked paprika
- ✓ Salt and pepper to taste

Step-by-Step Preparation:

1. Season the chicken drumsticks with garlic powder, smoked paprika, salt, and pepper.

2. Place them in the slow cooker and pour the chicken broth over them.

3. Dot the butter on top of the drumsticks.

4. Cover and cook on low for 6 hours, until the drumsticks are tender.

5. Serve the drumsticks with the rich, savory juices from the slow cooker.

Nutritional Facts: (Per serving)

- ❖ Calories: 320
- ❖ Protein: 27g
- ❖ Fat: 22g
- ❖ Carbohydrates: 1g

These Slow Cooker Chicken Drumsticks offer a simple, no-fuss way to enjoy a hearty carnivore meal. The combination of tender chicken and flavorful seasonings makes this dish perfect for any occasion, delivering a satisfying taste with minimal effort.

Recipe 14: Chicken Pot Pie

This hearty Chicken Pot Pie, made carnivore-style, is the perfect comfort food. With tender chicken, a rich creamy sauce, and savory bacon, this slow cooker version delivers all the flavors you love, without any of the carbs. It's a satisfying meal that's easy to make and perfect for any occasion.

Servings: 4

Prepping Time: 15 minutes

Cook Time: 6 hours

Difficulty: Medium

Ingredients:

- ✓ 4 boneless chicken thighs
- ✓ 8 oz cream cheese, softened
- ✓ 1/2 cup heavy cream
- ✓ 6 slices of bacon, cooked and crumbled
- ✓ 1/2 cup chicken broth
- ✓ 1 tsp garlic powder
- ✓ Salt and pepper to taste

Step-by-Step Preparation:

1. Place the chicken thighs in the slow cooker and season with garlic powder, salt, and pepper.

2. Add the cream cheese and chicken broth to the cooker.

3. Cover and cook on low for 6 hours until the chicken is tender.

4. Shred the chicken and stir in the heavy cream and crumbled bacon.

5. Let it cook for another 15 minutes to blend the flavors.

6. Serve hot with a ladle of the rich sauce.

Nutritional Facts: (Per serving)

- ❖ Calories: 450
- ❖ Protein: 32g
- ❖ Fat: 36g
- ❖ Carbohydrates: 2g

This slow-cooked Chicken Pot Pie is a carnivore diet twist on a classic, loaded with savory goodness. It's rich, creamy, and bursting with flavors that will leave you satisfied and craving more. Easy to prepare, this recipe makes a perfect meal for any day of the week.

Recipe 15: Chicken Taco With Corn

Enjoy the flavorful combination of tender chicken and sweet corn in these Carnivore Diet Chicken Tacos. This slow cooker recipe is easy to prepare and results in perfectly seasoned chicken, ideal for a low-carb meal packed with protein and wholesome flavors.

Servings: 4

Prepping Time: 10 minutes

Cook Time: 6 hours

Difficulty: Easy

Ingredients:

- ✓ 4 boneless, skinless chicken breasts
- ✓ 1 cup chicken broth
- ✓ 1 tsp garlic powder
- ✓ 1 tsp paprika
- ✓ Salt and pepper to taste
- ✓ 1 cup corn kernels (optional)

Step-by-Step Preparation:

1. Place the chicken breasts in the slow cooker and season with garlic powder, paprika, salt, and pepper.

2. Pour the chicken broth over the chicken and cover the slow cooker.

3. Cook on low for 6 hours until the chicken is tender.

4. Shred the chicken and mix in the corn kernels.

5. Serve the chicken in your favorite low-carb tortillas or lettuce wraps, topped with your choice of condiments.

Nutritional Facts: (Per serving)

- ❖ Calories: 350
- ❖ Protein: 30g
- ❖ Fat: 12g
- ❖ Carbohydrates: 8g

These Chicken Tacos with Corn are a simple yet satisfying way to enjoy taco night while following the carnivore diet. Packed with flavor and nutrition, this dish is easy to make and versatile enough to customize with your favorite toppings. Perfect for a hearty and delicious meal!

Recipe 16: Chicken With Seasoning Mix and Creamer Potatoes

This comforting Chicken Cooked in a Slow Cooker with Seasoning Mix and Creamer Potatoes is a carnivore-friendly dish that's easy to prepare and full of rich, hearty flavors. The chicken becomes tender and juicy while the creamer potatoes soak up the savory seasonings, making this meal satisfying and delicious.

Servings: 4

Prepping Time: 15 minutes

Cook Time: 6 hours

Difficulty: Easy

Ingredients:

- ✓ 4 boneless, skinless chicken thighs
- ✓ 1 lb creamer potatoes, halved

- ✓ 1 packet seasoning mix (e.g., garlic herb or ranch)
- ✓ 1/2 cup chicken broth
- ✓ Salt and pepper to taste

Step-by-Step Preparation:

1. Place the chicken thighs in the slow cooker and sprinkle the seasoning mix over them.

2. Add the halved creamer potatoes around the chicken.

3. Pour the chicken broth over the chicken and potatoes.

4. Season with additional salt and pepper if desired.

5. Cover and cook on low for 6 hours until the chicken is tender and the potatoes are soft.

6. Serve hot, spooning the flavorful broth over the chicken and potatoes.

Nutritional Facts: (Per serving)

- ❖ Calories: 400
- ❖ Protein: 30g

- ❖ Fat: 20g
- ❖ Carbohydrates: 18g

This slow cooker chicken and creamer potato dish delivers a comforting, protein-packed meal with minimal effort. The seasoning mix enhances the flavors of the tender chicken and creamy potatoes, making it perfect for any dinner. With just a few ingredients, this recipe is both satisfying and easy to prepare.

Recipe 17: Stuffed Pepper Sauce With Chicken Meat and Rice

Savor the deliciousness of tender chicken meat stuffed with rice, all covered in a rich roasted pepper sauce in this slow cooker carnivore-friendly recipe. The slow cooking method infuses every bite with deep, satisfying flavors, making it an ideal comfort meal that's both hearty and wholesome.

Servings: 4

Prepping Time: 20 minutes

Cook Time: 6 hours

Difficulty: Medium

Ingredients:

- ✓ 4 boneless chicken breasts
- ✓ 1 cup cooked rice
- ✓ 1/2 cup shredded cheese (optional)
- ✓ 1 tsp garlic powder
- ✓ Salt and pepper to taste
- ✓ 4 roasted red bell peppers, pureed
- ✓ 1/2 cup chicken broth
- ✓ 1 tsp paprika
- ✓ 2 tbsp olive oil

Step-by-Step Preparation:

1. Butterfly the chicken breasts and season with garlic powder, salt, and pepper.
2. Stuff the chicken breasts with the cooked rice and shredded cheese, then secure with toothpicks.
3. Place the stuffed chicken in the slow cooker.
4. In a bowl, mix the pureed roasted peppers, chicken broth, paprika, and olive oil, then pour over the chicken.
5. Cover and cook on low for 6 hours until the chicken is tender.
6. Serve with the roasted pepper sauce spooned over the stuffed chicken.

Nutritional Facts: (Per serving)

- ❖ Calories: 450
- ❖ Protein: 35g
- ❖ Fat: 20g
- ❖ Carbohydrates: 25g

This Stuffed Chicken with Rice and Roasted Pepper Sauce is a delicious and comforting carnivore meal. The slow cooker makes the chicken perfectly tender while the roasted pepper sauce adds a rich flavor. It's a hearty dish that's sure to satisfy your hunger and keep you coming back for more.

Recipe 18: Tender Chicken Fillet in a Creamy Mushroom Sauce

This slow-cooked tender chicken fillet in a creamy mushroom sauce with rice and green peas is the perfect comfort meal. Packed with savory flavors, this chicken stew with vegetables and a rich mushroom cream sauce is hearty, satisfying, and ideal for carnivore diet enthusiasts looking for a wholesome, protein-rich dish.

Servings: 4

Prepping Time: 15 minutes

Cook Time: 6 hours

Difficulty: Medium

Ingredients:

- ✓ 4 chicken fillets
- ✓ 1 cup sliced mushrooms
- ✓ 1/2 cup heavy cream
- ✓ 1/2 cup chicken broth
- ✓ 1 cup cooked rice
- ✓ 1/2 cup green peas
- ✓ 1 tsp garlic powder
- ✓ Salt and pepper to taste
- ✓ 1 tbsp olive oil

Step-by-Step Preparation:

1. Season the chicken fillets with garlic powder, salt, and pepper, then place them in the slow cooker.

2. Add the sliced mushrooms on top of the chicken.

3. Pour in the chicken broth and heavy cream, then cover the slow cooker.

4. Cook on low for 6 hours until the chicken is tender.

5. In the last 30 minutes, stir in the cooked rice and green peas.

6. Serve the tender chicken fillets with the creamy mushroom sauce over rice and peas.

Nutritional Facts: (Per serving)

- ❖ Calories: 480
- ❖ Protein: 38g
- ❖ Fat: 25g
- ❖ Carbohydrates: 28g

This hearty chicken stew with creamy mushroom sauce delivers a satisfying and flavorful meal that's perfect for any day. The slow cooking process ensures tender, juicy chicken with a rich, savory sauce that pairs beautifully with rice and peas. Simple to prepare, it's a great option for a nourishing dinner.

Recipe 19: Chicken Piccata With Sauce and Lemon

This Chicken Piccata with Sauce and Lemon brings a zesty twist to your carnivore diet. Slow-cooked to perfection, the chicken is tender and juicy, infused with the bright flavors of lemon and a rich buttery sauce. It's a simple yet elegant dish that makes for a refreshing and flavorful meal.

Servings: 4

Prepping Time: 10 minutes

Cook Time: 6 hours

Difficulty: Easy

Ingredients:

- ✓ 4 boneless, skinless chicken breasts
- ✓ 1/4 cup lemon juice (freshly squeezed)
- ✓ 1/2 cup chicken broth
- ✓ 2 tbsp capers (optional)
- ✓ 3 tbsp butter
- ✓ 1 tsp garlic powder
- ✓ Salt and pepper to taste

Step-by-Step Preparation:

1. Season the chicken breasts with garlic powder, salt, and pepper.

2. Place the chicken in the slow cooker and pour the chicken broth and lemon juice over it.

3. Add capers if desired and dot the butter on top of the chicken.

4. Cover and cook on low for 6 hours until the chicken is tender and infused with the lemony sauce.

5. Serve the chicken with a drizzle of the sauce from the slow cooker.

Nutritional Facts: (Per serving)

- ❖ Calories: 300
- ❖ Protein: 28g
- ❖ Fat: 18g
- ❖ Carbohydrates: 2g

This Chicken Piccata with Lemon and Sauce is a refreshing and light carnivore-friendly recipe that delivers bold flavors with minimal effort. The tangy lemon sauce perfectly complements the tender chicken, making it a dish you'll love for its simplicity and delicious taste.

Recipe 20: Creamy Chicken Curry Garnished With Parsley

This Creamy Chicken Curry garnished with parsley is a flavorful and satisfying dish for the carnivore diet. The rich, creamy sauce infused with aromatic spices makes the chicken tender and delicious. Slow-cooked to perfection, this recipe offers a comforting meal with a touch of fresh parsley to brighten every bite.

Servings: 4

Prepping Time: 10 minutes

Cook Time: 6 hours

Difficulty: Easy

Ingredients:

- ✓ 4 boneless, skinless chicken breasts
- ✓ 1 cup heavy cream
- ✓ 1/2 cup chicken broth
- ✓ 1 tbsp curry powder
- ✓ 1 tsp garlic powder
- ✓ Salt and pepper to taste
- ✓ Fresh parsley, chopped, for garnish

Step-by-Step Preparation:

1. Season the chicken breasts with curry powder, garlic powder, salt, and pepper.

2. Place the chicken in the slow cooker and pour in the chicken broth and heavy cream.

3. Cover and cook on low for 6 hours until the chicken is tender and the sauce is thick and creamy.

4. Garnish with freshly chopped parsley before serving.

Nutritional Facts: (Per serving)

- ❖ Calories: 380
- ❖ Protein: 30g
- ❖ Fat: 28g
- ❖ Carbohydrates: 2g

This Creamy Chicken Curry offers a rich, comforting meal that's perfect for those following a carnivore diet. The slow cooker makes the chicken tender, and the creamy curry sauce is packed with bold flavors. Garnished with parsley, it's an easy yet impressive dish that's sure to become a favorite.

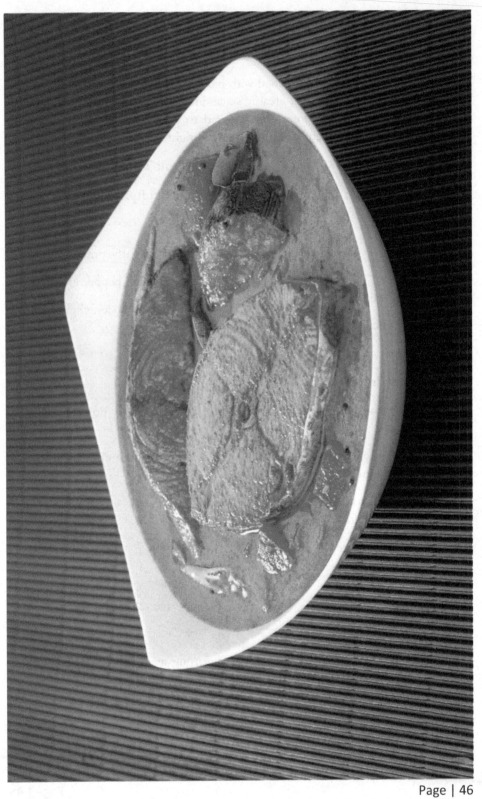

Chapter 03: Flavorful Fish

Recipe 21: Seer Fish Curry

Seer Fish Curry is a flavorful traditional Indian dish from Kerala, rich in spices and creamy coconut. This slow cooker version ensures tender, succulent fish, perfect for the Carnivore Diet. The aromatic curry is garnished with fresh curry leaves, offering a taste of Kerala's culinary heritage.

Servings: 4

Prepping Time: 15 minutes

Cook Time: 4 hours

Difficulty: Easy

Ingredients:

- 4 Seer fish fillets
- 1 cup coconut milk
- 2 tbsp coconut oil
- 1 tbsp turmeric powder
- 2 tbsp red chili powder
- 1 tsp black pepper
- 5-6 curry leaves
- 2 tbsp ginger-garlic paste
- Salt to taste

Step-by-Step Preparation:

1. In a slow cooker, heat coconut oil and sauté ginger-garlic paste.
2. Add turmeric, red chili powder, black pepper, and salt, stirring until fragrant.
3. Add coconut milk and stir well.
4. Place the seer fish fillets in the sauce.
5. Cook on low heat for 4 hours.
6. Garnish with fresh curry leaves before serving.

Nutritional Facts: (Per serving):

- Calories: 280
- Protein: 30g
- Fat: 18g
- Carbs: 4g

Enjoy this rich and flavorful Seer Fish Curry, a Kerala classic, ideal for anyone on a Carnivore Diet. The creamy coconut base perfectly complements the spices, leaving a lasting impression with each bite.

Recipe 22: Traditional Asian Fish Curry Dish

Traditional Asian Fish Curry brings a rich blend of aromatic spices and tender fish, creating a dish full of flavor and depth. This Carnivore Diet version, slow-cooked to perfection, provides a creamy, savory experience that is both satisfying and healthy.

Servings: 4

Prepping Time: 10 minutes

Cook Time: 4 hours

Difficulty: Easy

Ingredients:

- ✓ 4 firm white fish fillets (such as cod or halibut)
- ✓ 1 cup coconut milk
- ✓ 2 tbsp coconut oil
- ✓ 1 tbsp turmeric powder
- ✓ 1 tbsp ground ginger
- ✓ 1 tbsp garlic paste
- ✓ 2 tbsp fish sauce
- ✓ 1 tbsp lime juice
- ✓ Salt to taste
- ✓ Fresh coriander for garnish

Step-by-Step Preparation:

1. Heat coconut oil in a slow cooker and sauté garlic paste and ginger.

2. Add turmeric, fish sauce, lime juice, and coconut milk, stirring to combine.

3. Place the fish fillets in the slow cooker, ensuring they are submerged in the sauce.

4. Cook on low for 4 hours until the fish is tender and cooked through.

5. Garnish with fresh coriander before serving.

Nutritional Facts: (Per serving):

- ❖ Calories: 250
- ❖ Protein: 28g
- ❖ Fat: 15g
- ❖ Carbs: 3g

This Traditional Asian Fish Curry offers a simple yet exotic blend of flavors. The slow-cooking method ensures the fish absorbs the spices, creating a dish that's perfect for the Carnivore Diet, satisfying both your health and taste buds.

Recipe 23: Kerala Fish Curry Hot and Spicy Anchovy Masala

Kerala Fish Curry is a hot and spicy dish from Alappuzha, India, featuring anchovy cooked in a rich, flavorful masala gravy with coconut milk. This slow cooker version brings out the authentic taste of Indian spices, perfect for those on a Carnivore Diet.

Servings: 4

Prepping Time: 15 minutes

Cook Time: 4 hours

Difficulty: Easy

Ingredients:

- ✓ 500g anchovy (cleaned)
- ✓ 1 cup coconut milk
- ✓ 2 tbsp coconut oil
- ✓ 1 tbsp turmeric powder
- ✓ 2 tbsp red chili powder
- ✓ 1 tsp black pepper
- ✓ 1 tbsp garlic paste
- ✓ 1 tbsp ginger paste
- ✓ 5-6 curry leaves
- ✓ Salt to taste

Step-by-Step Preparation:

1. Heat coconut oil in a slow cooker, then add garlic paste, ginger paste, and curry leaves.

2. Stir in turmeric, red chili powder, black pepper, and salt, sautéing until fragrant.

3. Add coconut milk and stir to combine the spices.

4. Place the cleaned anchovies in the slow cooker, ensuring they are covered with the sauce.

5. Cook on low for 4 hours until the fish is tender.

6. Garnish with additional curry leaves before serving.

Nutritional Facts: (Per serving):

- ❖ Calories: 240
- ❖ Protein: 25g
- ❖ Fat: 16g
- ❖ Carbs: 2g

This Kerala Fish Curry, with its spicy and creamy gravy, is a true taste of Southern India. The slow-cooked anchovies absorb the intense flavors of the masala, offering a rich dish that fits perfectly into the Carnivore Diet, bringing spice and satisfaction to every bite.

Recipe 24: King or Barracuda Fish Curry

This hot and spicy Kerala King or Barracuda fish curry, made with coconut milk, is a true celebration of Southern Indian flavors. Slow-cooked for tenderness and infused with aromatic spices, it's a delicious addition to your Carnivore Diet meal plan.

Servings: 4

Prepping Time: 15 minutes

Cook Time: 4 hours

Difficulty: Easy

Ingredients:

- ✓ 4 King fish or Barracuda fillets
- ✓ 1 cup coconut milk
- ✓ 2 tbsp coconut oil
- ✓ 1 tbsp turmeric powder
- ✓ 2 tbsp red chili powder
- ✓ 1 tsp black pepper
- ✓ 1 tbsp garlic paste
- ✓ 1 tbsp ginger paste
- ✓ 5-6 curry leaves
- ✓ Salt to taste

Step-by-Step Preparation:

1. Heat coconut oil in a slow cooker and sauté garlic paste, ginger paste, and curry leaves until fragrant.

2. Add turmeric, red chili powder, black pepper, and salt, stirring well.

3. Pour in the coconut milk and mix thoroughly.

4. Place the Kingfish or Barracuda fillets in the sauce, ensuring they are covered.

5. Cook on low for 4 hours until the fish is tender.

6. Garnish with additional curry leaves before serving.

Nutritional Facts: (Per serving):

- ❖ Calories: 300
- ❖ Protein: 30g
- ❖ Fat: 20g
- ❖ Carbs: 3g

This Kerala King Fish or Barracuda curry is a flavorful, spicy dish that embodies the rich culinary traditions of Kerala. The coconut milk balances the heat of the spices, creating a satisfying and nutritious dish that fits perfectly with the Carnivore Diet. Enjoy this delightful slow-cooked curry!

Recipe 25: Spicy and Hot Pomfret Fish Curry

Spicy and hot Pomfret fish curry is a flavorful dish packed with aromatic spices, tender Pomfret fish, and creamy coconut milk. Slow-cooked to perfection with curry leaves, this Carnivore Diet recipe brings the essence of traditional Indian cooking to your kitchen.

Servings: 4

Cook Time: 4 hours

Prepping Time: 15 minutes

Difficulty: Easy

Ingredients:

- ✓ 4 Pomfret fish fillets
- ✓ 1 cup coconut milk
- ✓ 2 tbsp coconut oil
- ✓ 1 tbsp turmeric powder
- ✓ 2 tbsp red chili powder
- ✓ 1 tsp black pepper
- ✓ 1 tbsp ginger-garlic paste
- ✓ 5-6 curry leaves
- ✓ Salt to taste

Step-by-Step Preparation:

1. Heat coconut oil in a slow cooker and sauté ginger-garlic paste with curry leaves.
2. Add turmeric, red chili powder, black pepper, and salt, stirring until fragrant.
3. Pour in coconut milk and mix well.
4. Place Pomfret fish fillets in the slow cooker, ensuring they are submerged in the sauce.
5. Cook on low for 4 hours until the fish is tender.
6. Garnish with fresh curry leaves before serving.

Nutritional Facts: (Per serving):

- ❖ Calories: 260
- ❖ Protein: 28g
- ❖ Fat: 18g
- ❖ Carbs: 2g

This spicy and hot Pomfret fish curry offers a delightful blend of heat and creaminess, creating a comforting dish. Perfect for the Carnivore Diet, the slow cooking enhances the flavors, making each bite of the Pomfret fish tender and packed with traditional Indian spices. Enjoy this hearty meal!

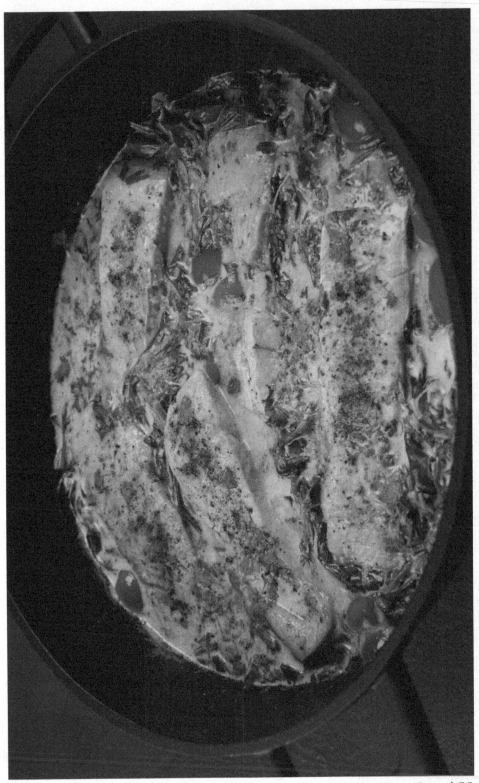

Recipe 26: Salmon Fillet With Spinach and Cherry Tomatoes

Salmon Fillet with Spinach and Cherry Tomatoes in Creamy Sauce is a deliciously rich and nutritious dish, perfect for the Carnivore Diet. The slow cooker brings out the tenderness of the salmon, while the creamy sauce enhances the flavors of spinach and tomatoes.

Servings: 4

Prepping Time: 10 minutes

Cook Time: 4 hours

Difficulty: Easy

Ingredients:

- ✓ 4 salmon fillets
- ✓ 1 cup heavy cream
- ✓ 1 tbsp butter
- ✓ 1 cup fresh spinach
- ✓ 1/2 cup cherry tomatoes, halved
- ✓ 1 tbsp garlic paste
- ✓ Salt and pepper to taste
- ✓ Fresh parsley for garnish

Step-by-Step Preparation:

1. Melt butter in a slow cooker and sauté garlic paste until fragrant.
2. Add heavy cream, spinach, and cherry tomatoes, stirring gently to combine.
3. Place the salmon fillets in the slow cooker, ensuring they are submerged in the sauce.
4. Season with salt and pepper to taste.
5. Cook on low for 4 hours until the salmon is tender and cooked through.
6. Garnish with fresh parsley before serving.

Nutritional Facts: (Per serving):

- ❖ Calories: 320
- ❖ Protein: 30g
- ❖ Fat: 22g
- ❖ Carbs: 4g

This Salmon Fillet with Spinach and Cherry Tomatoes in Creamy Sauce is a satisfying and flavorful dish that perfectly complements a Carnivore Diet. The slow cooking ensures the salmon stays tender, while the creamy sauce and veggies add a rich depth to the dish. Enjoy this easy, wholesome meal!

Recipe 27: Hilsa Fish Curry

Shorshe Ilish is a traditional Bengali dish made with tender Hilsa fish cooked in a rich, spicy mustard gravy and green chili. This slow cooker version preserves the authentic flavors while fitting perfectly into a Carnivore Diet plan.

Servings: 4

Prepping Time: 15 minutes

Cook Time: 4 hours

Difficulty: Medium

Ingredients:

- ✓ 4 Hilsa fish fillets
- ✓ 3 tbsp mustard paste
- ✓ 2 tbsp mustard oil
- ✓ 1/2 cup coconut milk
- ✓ 4-5 green chilies (slit)
- ✓ 1 tsp turmeric powder
- ✓ Salt to taste
- ✓ 1/2 cup water
- ✓ Fresh coriander for garnish

Step-by-Step Preparation:

1. Heat mustard oil in a slow cooker, then add the mustard paste and turmeric powder, sautéing until fragrant.

2. Add coconut milk, water, and salt, stirring well to form a smooth gravy.

3. Place the Hilsa fish fillets in the slow cooker and add green chilies.

4. Cook on low heat for 4 hours until the fish is tender and the flavors are infused.

5. Garnish with fresh coriander before serving.

Nutritional Facts: (Per serving):

- ❖ Calories: 280
- ❖ Protein: 28g
- ❖ Fat: 18g
- ❖ Carbs: 3g

Shorshe Ilish is a beloved Bengali delicacy, and this slow-cooked version enhances the dish's rich flavors while keeping the Hilsa fish moist and succulent. The mustard gravy, combined with the heat of green chilies, creates a bold and satisfying meal that is perfect for the Carnivore Diet. Enjoy this cultural favorite!

Recipe 28: Tilapia Fish With Red Curry Sauce

Shorshe Ilish is a traditional Bengali dish made with tender Hilsa fish cooked in rich, spicy mustard gravy and green chili. This slow cooker version preserves the authentic flavors while fitting perfectly into a Carnivore Diet plan.

Servings: 4

Prepping Time: 15 minutes

Cook Time: 4 hours

Difficulty: Medium

Ingredients:

- ✓ 4 Hilsa fish fillets
- ✓ 3 tbsp mustard paste
- ✓ 2 tbsp mustard oil
- ✓ 1/2 cup coconut milk
- ✓ 4-5 green chilies (slit)
- ✓ 1 tsp turmeric powder
- ✓ Salt to taste
- ✓ 1/2 cup water
- ✓ Fresh coriander for garnish

Step-by-Step Preparation:

1. Heat mustard oil in a slow cooker, then add the mustard paste and turmeric powder, sautéing until fragrant.

2. Add coconut milk, water, and salt, stirring well to form a smooth gravy.

3. Place the Hilsa fish fillets in the slow cooker and add green chilies.

4. Cook on low heat for 4 hours until the fish is tender and the flavors are infused.

5. Garnish with fresh coriander before serving.

Nutritional Facts: (Per serving):

- ❖ Calories: 280
- ❖ Protein: 28g
- ❖ Fat: 18g
- ❖ Carbs: 3g

Shorshe Ilish is a beloved Bengali delicacy, and this slow-cooked version enhances the dish's rich flavors while keeping the Hilsa fish moist and succulent. The mustard gravy, combined with the heat of green chilies, creates a bold and satisfying meal that is perfect for the Carnivore Diet. Enjoy this cultural favorite!

Recipe 29: Snapper Fish Curry

Gulai Ikan, a classic West Sumatran dish from Indonesia, is a rich and aromatic snapper fish curry cooked in a flavorful coconut sauce. This slow cooker version brings out the tender texture of the snapper while maintaining the authentic, spicy taste of the region, perfect for the Carnivore Diet.

Servings: 4

Prepping Time: 15 minutes

Cook Time: 4 hours

Difficulty: Easy

Ingredients:

- ✓ 4 snapper fillets
- ✓ 1 cup coconut milk
- ✓ 2 tbsp coconut oil
- ✓ 2 tbsp turmeric powder
- ✓ 2 tbsp red chili paste
- ✓ 1 tbsp ground coriander
- ✓ 1 tbsp garlic paste
- ✓ 1 tbsp ginger paste
- ✓ 5-6 kaffir lime leaves
- ✓ Salt to taste

Step-by-Step Preparation:

1. Heat coconut oil in a slow cooker and sauté garlic paste, ginger paste, and kaffir lime leaves.

2. Add turmeric powder, red chili paste, ground coriander, and salt, stirring until the spices are fragrant.

3. Stir in the coconut milk and mix well.

4. Place the snapper fillets in the slow cooker, ensuring they are covered in the sauce.

5. Cook on low for 4 hours until the fish is tender and the sauce is infused with flavor.

6. Garnish with additional kaffir lime leaves before serving.

Nutritional Facts: (Per serving):

- ❖ Calories: 290
- ❖ Protein: 32g
- ❖ Fat: 18g
- ❖ Carbs: 3g

Gulai Ikan offers a wonderful balance of bold spices and creamy coconut, creating a rich and flavorful dish. The slow cooking allows the snapper to absorb the deep, aromatic flavors, making it a delicious and satisfying meal for those following the Carnivore Diet. Savor the taste of West Sumatra!

Recipe 30: Hilsa Fish Cooking With Mustard Seed

Sorshe Ilish, or Hilsa fish cooked with mustard seeds, is a beloved Bengali delicacy known for its rich, bold flavors. This slow cooker version enhances the traditional taste of mustard and spices, making it a perfect Carnivore Diet dish that's both aromatic and delicious.

Servings: 4

Prepping Time: 15 minutes

Cook Time: 4 hours

Difficulty: Medium

Ingredients:

- ✓ 4 Hilsa fish fillets
- ✓ 3 tbsp mustard seeds (ground into a paste)
- ✓ 1/2 cup coconut milk
- ✓ 2 tbsp mustard oil
- ✓ 1 tsp turmeric powder
- ✓ 4-5 green chilies (slit)
- ✓ Salt to taste
- ✓ 1/2 cup water
- ✓ Fresh coriander for garnish

Step-by-Step Preparation:

1. In a slow cooker, heat mustard oil and add the mustard seed paste and turmeric powder. Sauté until fragrant.

2. Add coconut milk, water, and salt, stirring well to form a smooth gravy.

3. Place the Hilsa fish fillets in the slow cooker and add the green chilies.

4. Cook on low for 4 hours until the fish is tender and the mustard flavor is infused.

5. Garnish with fresh coriander before serving.

Nutritional Facts: (Per serving):

- ❖ Calories: 280
- ❖ Protein: 30g
- ❖ Fat: 18g
- ❖ Carbs: 2g

Sorshe Ilish is a true representation of Bengali cuisine, offering a unique and flavorful mustard gravy that perfectly complements the tender Hilsa fish. This slow cooker recipe allows the spices to meld beautifully, providing a satisfying and nutritious meal for those on the Carnivore Diet. Enjoy the authentic taste of Bengal!

Chapter 04: Succulent Seafood

Recipe 31: Fish Stew Cioppino With Prawns

Traditional American fish stew, Cioppino, is a delightful seafood dish rich with prawns and fish, perfect for the Carnivore Diet. Its slow cooker method ensures tender, flavorful results, allowing the seafood to absorb all the delicious seasonings while keeping the dish simple and hassle-free.

Servings: 4

Prepping Time: 15 minutes

Cook Time: 6 hours

Difficulty: Easy

Ingredients:

- ✓ 1 pound of prawns, peeled and deveined
- ✓ 1 pound of white fish fillets (such as cod or haddock), cut into chunks
- ✓ 2 cups of fish stock
- ✓ 1 onion, chopped
- ✓ 4 cloves of garlic, minced
- ✓ 1 teaspoon of sea salt
- ✓ 1/2 teaspoon of black pepper
- ✓ 1 tablespoon of fresh parsley, chopped

Step-by-Step Preparation:

1. In the slow cooker, add the prawns and fish fillets.
2. Pour in the fish stock, ensuring the seafood is covered.
3. Add the chopped onion, minced garlic, salt, and pepper.
4. Stir gently to combine the ingredients.
5. Set the slow cooker on low and cook for 6 hours.
6. Before serving, sprinkle fresh parsley over the stew for garnish.

Nutritional Facts (Per serving):

- ❖ Calories: 280
- ❖ Protein: 35g
- ❖ Fat: 12g
- ❖ Carbohydrates: 0g
- ❖ Sodium: 400mg

This hearty Cioppino stew is a nourishing option for those on a Carnivore Diet, offering high-quality protein and flavors that will leave you feeling satisfied. Perfect for a cozy meal, it's easy to prepare and a great way to enjoy seafood at its best.

Recipe 32: Marinated Abalone in Soy Sauce

Marinated abalone in soy sauce with red and green peppers is a flavorful and delicate seafood dish, perfect for the Carnivore Diet. The slow cooker method ensures tender abalone, while the soy sauce marinade enhances its rich taste, complemented by vibrant peppers.

Servings: 4

Prepping Time: 20 minutes

Cook Time: 4 hours

Difficulty: Easy

Ingredients:

- ✓ 8 pieces of fresh abalone
- ✓ 1/4 cup soy sauce
- ✓ 1 tablespoon sesame oil
- ✓ 2 cloves garlic, minced
- ✓ 1 red pepper, sliced
- ✓ 1 green pepper, sliced
- ✓ 1 teaspoon sea salt
- ✓ 1/2 teaspoon black pepper

Step-by-Step Preparation:

1. In a bowl, combine soy sauce, sesame oil, garlic, salt, and pepper.
2. Add the abalone to the marinade and let it sit for 15 minutes.
3. Place the marinated abalone and sliced peppers into the slow cooker.
4. Pour any remaining marinade over the abalone.
5. Set the slow cooker to low and cook for 4 hours, until the abalone is tender.
6. Serve hot, garnished with extra peppers if desired.

Nutritional Facts (Per serving):

- ❖ Calories: 150
- ❖ Protein: 18g
- ❖ Fat: 5g
- ❖ Carbohydrates: 2g
- ❖ Sodium: 620mg

This marinated abalone dish brings out the rich, umami flavors of soy sauce with a tender, melt-in-your-mouth texture. A simple yet elegant seafood recipe, it's perfect for those following a Carnivore Diet, offering a savory experience that's both satisfying and nourishing.

Recipe 33: Stewed Squid Rings in Tomato Sauce

Stewed squid rings in tomato sauce is a delicious and hearty Carnivore Diet dish, packed with flavor and nutrients. The squid becomes tender through slow cooking, while the tomato sauce infuses the dish with a rich, savory taste, making it a perfect seafood meal.

Servings: 4

Prepping Time: 15 minutes

Cook Time: 4 hours

Difficulty: Easy

Ingredients:

- ✓ 1-pound squid rings
- ✓ 2 cups tomato sauce
- ✓ 1 onion, finely chopped
- ✓ 4 cloves garlic, minced
- ✓ 1 teaspoon sea salt
- ✓ 1/2 teaspoon black pepper
- ✓ 1 tablespoon olive oil
- ✓ 1 teaspoon fresh basil, chopped (optional)

Step-by-Step Preparation:

1. Heat olive oil in a pan and sauté the onion and garlic until softened.

2. Add squid rings and cook for 3-4 minutes until lightly seared.

3. Transfer the squid, sautéed onions, and garlic into the slow cooker.

4. Pour in the tomato sauce and season with salt, pepper, and basil.

5. Set the slow cooker to low and cook for 4 hours until the squid is tender.

6. Serve hot, garnished with fresh basil if desired.

Nutritional Facts (Per serving):

- ❖ Calories: 220
- ❖ Protein: 25g
- ❖ Fat: 8g
- ❖ Carbohydrates: 6g
- ❖ Sodium: 600mg

This stewed squid ring in tomato sauce is a simple yet flavorful dish that combines the tenderness of squid with the richness of tomato sauce. Perfect for those on a Carnivore Diet, this satisfying seafood recipe offers a healthy, protein-packed meal with minimal effort.

Recipe 34: Thai Shrimp Green Curry

Thai Shrimp Green Curry is a flavorful and aromatic seafood dish, perfect for the Carnivore Diet. This slow-cooked version brings out the rich, spicy, and creamy flavors of green curry, enhancing the tenderness of shrimp for a satisfying and nutrient-rich meal.

Servings: 4

Prepping Time: 10 minutes

Cook Time: 3 hours

Difficulty: Easy

Ingredients:

- ✓ 1 pound shrimp, peeled and deveined
- ✓ 1 cup coconut milk
- ✓ 2 tablespoons green curry paste
- ✓ 1 tablespoon fish sauce
- ✓ 2 cloves garlic, minced
- ✓ 1 tablespoon olive oil
- ✓ 1/2 teaspoon sea salt
- ✓ 1/4 teaspoon black pepper
- ✓ 1 tablespoon lime juice
- ✓ Fresh basil leaves for garnish (optional)

Step-by-Step Preparation:

1. In a pan, heat olive oil and sauté the garlic until fragrant.

2. Add the green curry paste and stir for 1-2 minutes.

3. Transfer the curry paste mixture to the slow cooker.

4. Add the shrimp, coconut milk, fish sauce, salt, and pepper to the slow cooker.

5. Set the slow cooker on low and cook for 3 hours.

6. Stir in lime juice before serving and garnish with fresh basil leaves if desired.

Nutritional Facts (Per serving):

- ❖ Calories: 230
- ❖ Protein: 24g
- ❖ Fat: 14g
- ❖ Carbohydrates: 4g
- ❖ Sodium: 700mg

This Thai Shrimp Green Curry is a vibrant dish that showcases the fresh flavors of shrimp and creamy coconut milk. Ideal for those on a Carnivore Diet, it's a fragrant and satisfying meal that brings the taste of Thailand to your table with minimal effort.

Recipe 35: Shrimp Prawn Curry

Shrimp Prawn Curry is a delicious, protein-packed seafood dish that's perfect for the Carnivore Diet. Slow-cooking the shrimp and prawns in a rich, aromatic curry sauce brings out deep flavors, making this dish both satisfying and easy to prepare.

Servings: 4

Cook Time: 3 hours

Prepping Time: 15 minutes

Difficulty: Easy

Ingredients:

- ✓ 1 pound shrimp, peeled and deveined
- ✓ 1 pound prawns, peeled and deveined
- ✓ 1 cup coconut milk
- ✓ 2 tablespoons curry powder
- ✓ 1 tablespoon fish sauce
- ✓ 1 onion, finely chopped
- ✓ 3 cloves garlic, minced
- ✓ 1 tablespoon olive oil
- ✓ 1 teaspoon sea salt
- ✓ 1/2 teaspoon black pepper

Step-by-Step Preparation:

1. Heat olive oil in a pan and sauté the onion and garlic until softened.
2. Add the curry powder and stir for 2 minutes to release the flavors.
3. Transfer the onion mixture to the slow cooker.
4. Add the shrimp, prawns, coconut milk, fish sauce, salt, and pepper.
5. Set the slow cooker on low and cook for 3 hours.
6. Stir occasionally, and once cooked, serve hot.

Nutritional Facts (Per serving):

- ❖ Calories: 260
- ❖ Protein: 32g
- ❖ Fat: 12g
- ❖ Carbohydrates: 3g
- ❖ Sodium: 650mg

This Shrimp Prawn Curry is a perfect blend of seafood and spices, making it an irresistible dish for seafood lovers following the Carnivore Diet. The slow cooker ensures the shrimp and prawns remain tender while soaking up all the curry's rich, savory flavors. Enjoy a hearty, satisfying meal with minimal effort.

Recipe 36: Curry With Scallops and Rice

Indonesian Curry with Scallops and Rice is a flavorful, aromatic dish perfect for the Carnivore Diet. The slow-cooked scallops soak up the rich, spiced curry sauce, creating a savory and satisfying meal that's easy to prepare and packed with protein.

Servings: 4

Cook Time: 4 hours

Prepping Time: 15 minutes

Difficulty: Easy

Ingredients:

- ✓ 1 pound scallops
- ✓ 1 cup coconut milk
- ✓ 2 tablespoons Indonesian curry paste
- ✓ 1 tablespoon fish sauce
- ✓ 1 tablespoon olive oil
- ✓ 1 onion, finely chopped
- ✓ 3 cloves garlic, minced
- ✓ 1/2 teaspoon sea salt
- ✓ 1/4 teaspoon black pepper
- ✓ Fresh basil leaves (optional)

Step-by-Step Preparation:

1. Heat olive oil in a pan and sauté the onion and garlic until softened.

2. Stir in the Indonesian curry paste and cook for 2 minutes to release the flavors.

3. Transfer the onion mixture to the slow cooker.

4. Add the scallops, coconut milk, fish sauce, salt, and pepper.

5. Set the slow cooker on low and cook for 4 hours.

6. Serve with rice if desired, and garnish with fresh basil leaves.

Nutritional Facts (Per serving):

- ❖ Calories: 240
- ❖ Protein: 25g
- ❖ Fat: 14g
- ❖ Carbohydrates: 4g
- ❖ Sodium: 580mg

This Indonesian Curry with Scallops is a delicious fusion of rich flavors and tender seafood, making it an ideal meal for the Carnivore Diet. The slow cooker locks in the spices, enhancing the dish's depth while keeping the scallops tender and juicy. Perfect for a unique, comforting seafood dinner.

Recipe 37: Buttered Shrimp With Corn

Buttered Shrimp with Corn is a delightful Indonesian dish featuring tender shrimp and sweet corn, slow-cooked in a rich, buttery garlic sauce with spices. This Carnivore Diet-friendly recipe offers a perfect balance of flavors, making it a simple yet satisfying seafood meal.

Servings: 4

Prepping Time: 10 minutes

Cook Time: 3 hours

Difficulty: Easy

Ingredients:

- ✓ 1 pound shrimp, peeled and deveined
- ✓ 1 cup corn kernels (fresh or frozen)
- ✓ 1/2 cup butter
- ✓ 4 cloves garlic, minced
- ✓ 1 teaspoon paprika
- ✓ 1 teaspoon sea salt
- ✓ 1/2 teaspoon black pepper
- ✓ 1 tablespoon lemon juice
- ✓ 1 tablespoon fresh parsley, chopped (optional)

Step-by-Step Preparation:

1. In a skillet, melt the butter over medium heat and sauté garlic until fragrant.
2. Add shrimp, paprika, salt, and pepper, stirring for 2 minutes.
3. Transfer the shrimp mixture and corn to the slow cooker.
4. Set the slow cooker to low and cook for 3 hours, stirring occasionally.
5. Before serving, drizzle with lemon juice and garnish with fresh parsley.

Nutritional Facts (Per serving):

- ❖ Calories: 300
- ❖ Protein: 24g
- ❖ Fat: 20g
- ❖ Carbohydrates: 5g
- ❖ Sodium: 600mg

This Buttered Shrimp with Corn is a simple, flavorful meal that brings out the sweetness of corn and the rich taste of butter and shrimp. Perfect for a quick and satisfying Carnivore Diet dish, it offers a delicious balance of nutrients with minimal effort for a hearty seafood feast.

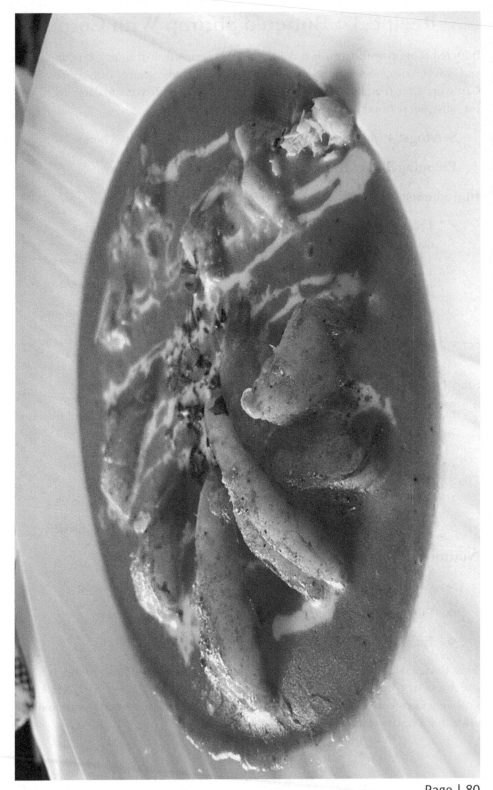

Recipe 38: Seafood Pan Roast

Seafood Pan Roast is a luxurious dish combining shrimp, crab meat, and lobster in a rich, creamy tomato sauce. This slow-cooked Carnivore Diet recipe offers a savory and indulgent meal, bringing out the best of seafood flavors with minimal effort.

Servings: 4

Prepping Time: 15 minutes

Cook Time: 4 hours

Difficulty: Easy

Ingredients:

- ✓ 1/2 pound shrimp, peeled and deveined
- ✓ 1/2 pound crab meat
- ✓ 1/2 pound lobster, cooked and chopped
- ✓ 2 cups tomato sauce
- ✓ 1 cup heavy cream
- ✓ 4 cloves garlic, minced
- ✓ 1 tablespoon olive oil
- ✓ 1 teaspoon sea salt
- ✓ 1/2 teaspoon black pepper
- ✓ 1 tablespoon fresh parsley, chopped (optional)

Step-by-Step Preparation:

1. Heat olive oil in a pan and sauté garlic until fragrant.

2. Add tomato sauce, cream, salt, and pepper, and stir until well combined.

3. Transfer the sauce to the slow cooker.

4. Add shrimp, crab meat, and lobster to the slow cooker.

5. Set the slow cooker on low and cook for 4 hours.

6. Before serving, garnish with fresh parsley if desired.

Nutritional Facts (Per serving):

- ❖ Calories: 450
- ❖ Protein: 36g
- ❖ Fat: 28g
- ❖ Carbohydrates: 8g
- ❖ Sodium: 850mg

This Seafood Pan Roast offers a rich, creamy, and indulgent seafood experience perfect for the Carnivore Diet. The slow-cooked shrimp, crab, and lobster soak up the flavors of the creamy tomato sauce, creating a hearty, satisfying dish that's perfect for a special occasion or any day you crave something luxurious.

Recipe 39: Pumpkin Puree Soup With Seafood

Pumpkin Purée Soup with Pumpkin Seeds, Seafood, Mussels, Shrimps, and Blue Cheese is a rich and creamy Carnivore Diet dish. This slow-cooked recipe combines the sweetness of pumpkin with savory seafood and the bold flavor of blue cheese for a truly satisfying meal.

Servings: 4

Prepping Time: 15 minutes

Cook Time: 4 hours

Difficulty: Easy

Ingredients:

- ✓ 1 pound shrimp, peeled and deveined
- ✓ 1 pound mussels, cleaned
- ✓ 4 cups pumpkin purée
- ✓ 2 cups seafood stock
- ✓ 1/2 cup blue cheese, crumbled
- ✓ 1/4 cup pumpkin seeds
- ✓ 2 cloves garlic, minced
- ✓ 1 teaspoon sea salt
- ✓ 1/2 teaspoon black pepper
- ✓ 1 tablespoon olive oil

Step-by-Step Preparation:

1. Heat olive oil in a pan and sauté garlic until fragrant.
2. Add the pumpkin purée and seafood stock, stirring well.
3. Transfer the mixture to the slow cooker and add shrimp and mussels.
4. Season with salt and pepper, and set the slow cooker on low for 4 hours.
5. Stir in the crumbled blue cheese before serving, and sprinkle with pumpkin seeds for garnish.

Nutritional Facts (Per serving):

- ❖ Calories: 350
- ❖ Protein: 28g
- ❖ Fat: 18g
- ❖ Carbohydrates: 10g
- ❖ Sodium: 720mg

This Pumpkin Purée Soup with seafood and blue cheese offers a delicious blend of sweet and savory flavors, making it a hearty meal for those following a Carnivore Diet. The seafood and cheese bring richness to the dish, while pumpkin seeds add a delightful crunch, perfect for a cozy, nutrient-packed meal.

Recipe 40: Moqueca With Fish and Shrimps

Moqueca is a traditional Brazilian seafood curry made with fish and shrimp, simmered in coconut milk and vegetables. This rich and flavorful dish, perfect for the Carnivore Diet, brings together tender seafood with a creamy, spiced sauce for an unforgettable meal.

Servings: 4

Cook Time: 4 hours

Prepping Time: 20 minutes

Difficulty: Easy

Ingredients:

- ✓ 1 pound white fish fillets (such as cod), cut into chunks
- ✓ 1 pound shrimp, peeled and deveined
- ✓ 1 cup coconut milk
- ✓ 1 onion, chopped
- ✓ 2 bell peppers (red and yellow), sliced
- ✓ 4 cloves garlic, minced
- ✓ 2 tomatoes, chopped
- ✓ 1 tablespoon olive oil
- ✓ 1 tablespoon lime juice
- ✓ 1 teaspoon paprika
- ✓ 1 teaspoon sea salt
- ✓ 1/2 teaspoon black pepper
- ✓ Fresh cilantro for garnish

Step-by-Step Preparation:

1. Heat olive oil in a pan and sauté onion, garlic, and bell peppers until softened.
2. Add tomatoes, paprika, salt, and pepper, stirring for 2-3 minutes.
3. Transfer the sautéed mixture to the slow cooker.
4. Add fish chunks, shrimp, and coconut milk, mixing gently to combine.
5. Set the slow cooker on low and cook for 4 hours.
6. Before serving, drizzle with lime juice and garnish with fresh cilantro.

Nutritional Facts (Per serving):

- ❖ Calories: 320
- ❖ Protein: 35g
- ❖ Fat: 18g
- ❖ Carbohydrates: 8g
- ❖ Sodium: 620mg

Moqueca with Fish and Shrimp is a vibrant, hearty dish that delivers the rich flavors of Brazilian cuisine in a simple, slow-cooked form. This seafood curry, with its creamy coconut base and tender fish, is perfect for those on the Carnivore Diet, offering a balanced, nutrient-packed meal that's both comforting and exotic.

Chapter 05: Hearty Soups

Recipe 41: Slow Cooker Chicken Taco Soup

This Slow Cooker Chicken Taco Soup is a hearty, flavorful dish that's perfect for the Carnivore Diet. Packed with tender chicken and rich spices, this soup is topped with fresh cilantro for a burst of freshness. It's a low-effort, nutrient-rich meal that slow cooks to perfection, ideal for any day of the week.

Servings: 4

Prepping Time: 10 minutes

Cook Time: 6-8 hours

Difficulty: Easy

Ingredients:

- ✓ 2 chicken breasts, boneless and skinless
- ✓ 4 cups chicken broth
- ✓ 1 cup diced tomatoes
- ✓ 1 cup chopped bell peppers
- ✓ 1 onion, chopped
- ✓ 1 tsp cumin
- ✓ 1 tsp chili powder
- ✓ 1 tsp paprika
- ✓ Salt and pepper to taste
- ✓ Fresh cilantro for topping

Step-by-Step Preparation:

1. Place the chicken breasts in the slow cooker.
2. Add the chicken broth, diced tomatoes, bell peppers, and onion.
3. Sprinkle cumin, chili powder, paprika, salt, and pepper over the ingredients.
4. Set the slow cooker to low and cook for 6-8 hours until the chicken is tender.
5. Shred the chicken using two forks and stir it back into the soup.
6. Serve hot and garnish with fresh cilantro.

Nutritional Facts: (Per serving):

- ❖ Calories: 220
- ❖ Protein: 25g
- ❖ Fat: 8g
- ❖ Carbohydrates: 5g
- ❖ Fiber: 2g

This Slow Cooker Chicken Taco Soup is an easy, nutritious meal that will keep you satisfied while adhering to the Carnivore Diet. The fresh cilantro topping adds a zesty finish to this slow-cooked delight, making it a wholesome choice for busy days.

Recipe 42: Indonesian chunky beef soup (Soto)

Savor the rich flavors of this Indonesian Chunky Beef Soup (Soto), a hearty, nourishing dish that's perfect for the Carnivore Diet. Slow-cooked to tender perfection, this soup blends bold spices and chunks of beef for a satisfying meal that warms the soul, all while keeping it low-carb and nutrient-dense.

Servings: 4

Cook Time: 6-8 hours

Prepping Time: 15 minutes

Difficulty: Easy

Ingredients:

- ✓ 1 lb beef chunks (stew meat)
- ✓ 4 cups beef broth
- ✓ 1 onion, chopped
- ✓ 4 garlic cloves, minced
- ✓ 2 tbsp ginger, minced
- ✓ 1 tsp turmeric
- ✓ 1 tsp cumin
- ✓ Salt and pepper to taste
- ✓ Fresh cilantro for garnish

Step-by-Step Preparation:

1. Place the beef chunks into the slow cooker.
2. Add the beef broth, chopped onion, minced garlic, and ginger.
3. Sprinkle turmeric, cumin, salt, and pepper over the ingredients.
4. Set the slow cooker to low and cook for 6-8 hours until the beef is tender.
5. Stir and adjust seasonings if necessary.
6. Serve hot, garnished with fresh cilantro.

Nutritional Facts: (Per serving):

- ❖ Calories: 290
- ❖ Protein: 30g
- ❖ Fat: 15g
- ❖ Carbohydrates: 3g
- ❖ Fiber: 1g

This Indonesian Chunky Beef Soup (Soto) offers a delightful blend of robust flavors with tender beef and warming spices. It's a simple yet comforting dish, perfect for those following a Carnivore Diet, and is an easy slow-cooker meal that will leave you satisfied and nourished.

Recipe 43: Chicken Taco Soup

This Chicken Taco Soup is a flavorful, hearty meal that fits perfectly into the Carnivore Diet. Topped with fresh cilantro and avocado, this slow-cooked soup is rich in protein and healthy fats. With minimal prep and a blend of tasty spices, it's a satisfying dish for any day of the week.

Servings: 4

Prepping Time: 10 minutes

Cook Time: 6-8 hours

Difficulty: Easy

Ingredients:

- ✓ 2 boneless, skinless chicken breasts
- ✓ 4 cups chicken broth
- ✓ 1 cup diced tomatoes
- ✓ 1 small onion, chopped
- ✓ 1 tsp cumin
- ✓ 1 tsp chili powder
- ✓ 1 tsp paprika
- ✓ Salt and pepper to taste
- ✓ Fresh cilantro for garnish
- ✓ 1 avocado, sliced for topping

Step-by-Step Preparation:

1. Place the chicken breasts in the slow cooker.

2. Add chicken broth, diced tomatoes, chopped onion, cumin, chili powder, paprika, salt, and pepper.

3. Set the slow cooker to low and cook for 6-8 hours, until the chicken is tender.

4. Shred the chicken using two forks and mix it back into the soup.

5. Serve hot, topped with fresh cilantro and avocado slices.

Nutritional Facts: (Per serving):

- ❖ Calories: 250
- ❖ Protein: 28g
- ❖ Fat: 12g
- ❖ Carbohydrates: 5g
- ❖ Fiber: 3g

This Chicken Taco Soup, enhanced with fresh cilantro and creamy avocado, is a nourishing, easy-to-make dish for anyone on the Carnivore Diet. Packed with protein and healthy fats, it's a convenient and delicious meal that's sure to satisfy. Perfect for slow cooker enthusiasts!

Recipe 44: Tuscany Sausage Gnocchi Bean Soup

This hearty Tuscany Sausage Gnocchi Bean Soup is a flavorful, slow-cooked delight tailored for the Carnivore Diet. Loaded with savory sausage, soft gnocchi, and rich broth, this soup brings the essence of Tuscany to your table. Easy to prepare, it's a satisfying and comforting dish for any occasion.

Servings: 4

Prepping Time: 15 minutes

Cook Time: 6-8 hours

Difficulty: Easy

Ingredients:

- ✓ 1 lb Italian sausage, ground
- ✓ 1 cup gnocchi
- ✓ 4 cups beef broth
- ✓ 1 cup white beans, cooked
- ✓ 1 onion, chopped
- ✓ 2 garlic cloves, minced
- ✓ 1 tsp dried basil
- ✓ 1 tsp oregano
- ✓ Salt and pepper to taste
- ✓ Fresh parsley for garnish

Step-by-Step Preparation:

1. Brown the sausage in a skillet, then transfer to the slow cooker.

2. Add beef broth, white beans, chopped onion, minced garlic, basil, oregano, salt, and pepper.

3. Set the slow cooker on low and cook for 6-8 hours.

4. Stir in the gnocchi during the last 30 minutes of cooking.

5. Serve hot and garnish with fresh parsley.

Nutritional Facts: (Per serving):

- ❖ Calories: 320
- ❖ Protein: 24g
- ❖ Fat: 15g
- ❖ Carbohydrates: 20g
- ❖ Fiber: 4g

This Tuscany Sausage Gnocchi Bean Soup is a perfect blend of savory flavors that's both rich and satisfying. Slow-cooked to perfection, the soft gnocchi and hearty sausage make for a delicious meal that fits seamlessly into the Carnivore Diet, offering a taste of Italy with every bite.

Recipe 45: Ham and Cannellini Bean Soup

This Ham and Cannellini Bean Soup is a rich, hearty meal that perfectly aligns with the Carnivore Diet. Slow-cooked to bring out deep flavors, the tender ham pairs wonderfully with cannellini beans for a satisfying, protein-packed soup that is easy to prepare and full of comforting flavors.

Servings: 4

Prepping Time: 10 minutes

Cook Time: 6-8 hours

Difficulty: Easy

Ingredients:

- ✓ 1 lb ham, diced
- ✓ 1 cup dried cannellini beans (soaked overnight)
- ✓ 4 cups chicken broth
- ✓ 1 onion, chopped
- ✓ 2 garlic cloves, minced
- ✓ 1 bay leaf
- ✓ 1 tsp thyme
- ✓ Salt and pepper to taste
- ✓ Fresh parsley for garnish

Step-by-Step Preparation:

1. Place the soaked cannellini beans and diced ham in the slow cooker.
2. Add chicken broth, chopped onion, minced garlic, bay leaf, thyme, salt, and pepper.
3. Set the slow cooker to low and cook for 6-8 hours until the beans are tender and the ham is fully cooked.
4. Stir and adjust seasoning if needed.
5. Serve hot, garnished with fresh parsley.

Nutritional Facts: (Per serving):

- ❖ Calories: 290
- ❖ Protein: 26g
- ❖ Fat: 12g
- ❖ Carbohydrates: 15g
- ❖ Fiber: 5g

This Ham and Cannellini Bean Soup is a simple yet flavorful dish, packed with protein and perfect for the Carnivore Diet. With tender ham and hearty beans in every bite, this slow-cooked soup offers a comforting and nutritious meal that's easy to make and delicious to enjoy.

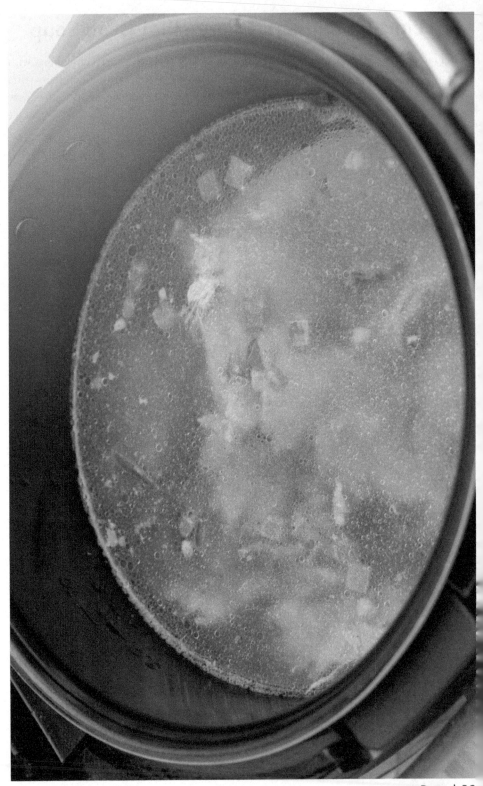

Recipe 46: Turkey Soup With Steamed Vegetables

This Turkey Soup with Steamed Vegetables is a wholesome and hearty option for those on the Carnivore Diet. Slow-cooked turkey paired with tender, steamed vegetables creates a flavorful and nutritious soup that's easy to prepare and packed with protein. Perfect for a satisfying and healthy meal any time of the week.

Servings: 4

Prepping Time: 15 minutes

Cook Time: 6-8 hours

Difficulty: Easy

Ingredients:

- ✓ 1 lb turkey breast, diced
- ✓ 4 cups turkey broth
- ✓ 1 cup carrots, sliced
- ✓ 1 cup zucchini, sliced
- ✓ 1 cup broccoli florets
- ✓ 1 onion, chopped
- ✓ 2 garlic cloves, minced
- ✓ 1 tsp thyme
- ✓ Salt and pepper to taste
- ✓ Fresh parsley for garnish

Step-by-Step Preparation:

1. Place the diced turkey breast in the slow cooker.
2. Add turkey broth, chopped onion, minced garlic, thyme, salt, and pepper.
3. Set the slow cooker to low and cook for 6-8 hours until the turkey is tender.
4. Steam the carrots, zucchini, and broccoli separately.
5. Add the steamed vegetables to the soup just before serving.
6. Serve hot, garnished with fresh parsley.

Nutritional Facts: (Per serving):

- ❖ Calories: 240
- ❖ Protein: 30g
- ❖ Fat: 8g
- ❖ Carbohydrates: 10g
- ❖ Fiber: 4g

This Turkey Soup with Steamed Vegetables is a nutrient-packed, flavorful meal ideal for the Carnivore Diet. The slow-cooked turkey, combined with tender steamed vegetables, delivers a hearty and satisfying dish that's both healthy and easy to prepare, making it a perfect choice for busy days.

Recipe 47: Chicken Soup With Rice

This Chicken Soup with Rice is a comforting, protein-rich meal perfect for the Carnivore Diet. Slowly cooked to perfection, this dish combines tender chicken and savory rice in a rich broth, creating a simple yet hearty meal that's ideal for any time of the day.

Servings: 4

Prepping Time: 10 minutes

Cook Time: 6-8 hours

Difficulty: Easy

Ingredients:

- ✓ 2 boneless, skinless chicken breasts
- ✓ 1 cup uncooked rice
- ✓ 4 cups chicken broth
- ✓ 1 onion, chopped
- ✓ 2 garlic cloves, minced
- ✓ 1 tsp thyme
- ✓ Salt and pepper to taste
- ✓ Fresh parsley for garnish

Step-by-Step Preparation:

1. Place the chicken breasts in the slow cooker.

2. Add chicken broth, chopped onion, minced garlic, thyme, salt, and pepper.

3. Set the slow cooker on low and cook for 6-8 hours until the chicken is tender.

4. About 30 minutes before serving, add the uncooked rice to the slow cooker.

5. Shred the chicken with two forks and stir it into the soup.

6. Serve hot, garnished with fresh parsley.

Nutritional Facts: (Per serving):

- ❖ Calories: 280
- ❖ Protein: 30g
- ❖ Fat: 6g
- ❖ Carbohydrates: 25g
- ❖ Fiber: 1g

This Chicken Soup with Rice is a warm, nourishing meal that's easy to make and perfect for those following a Carnivore Diet. The slow-cooked chicken paired with tender rice creates a satisfying dish that's ideal for cold days or a cozy family dinner.

Recipe 48: Fish Soup From Salmon

This Fish Soup made with salmon, potatoes, leek, and sour cream is a flavorful and creamy delight perfect for the Carnivore Diet. Slow-cooked to bring out the richness of the salmon and topped with fresh dill, this soup offers a comforting, nutritious meal that's easy to prepare and enjoy.

Servings: 4

Prepping Time: 15 minutes

Cook Time: 6-8 hours

Difficulty: Easy

Ingredients:

- ✓ 1 lb salmon fillet, diced
- ✓ 3 potatoes, peeled and chopped
- ✓ 1 leek, sliced
- ✓ 4 cups fish or vegetable broth
- ✓ 1 cup sour cream
- ✓ Salt and pepper to taste
- ✓ Fresh dill for garnish

Step-by-Step Preparation:

1. Place the diced salmon, chopped potatoes, and sliced leek in the slow cooker.

2. Add the broth, salt, and pepper.

3. Set the slow cooker to low and cook for 6-8 hours until the potatoes are tender and the salmon is fully cooked.

4. Stir in the sour cream just before serving.

5. Serve hot, topped with fresh dill.

Nutritional Facts: (Per serving):

- ❖ Calories: 320
- ❖ Protein: 25g
- ❖ Fat: 18g
- ❖ Carbohydrates: 12g
- ❖ Fiber: 2g

This salmon-based fish soup is a hearty and creamy dish that perfectly balances the richness of sour cream and the freshness of dill. It's an easy, slow-cooked recipe that delivers both nutrition and flavor, making it an ideal meal for anyone following the Carnivore Diet.

Recipe 49: Meatball Soup With Vegetables

This Meatball Soup with Vegetables is a hearty and nutritious Carnivore Diet recipe. The slow-cooked meatballs, combined with flavorful vegetables, create a delicious, comforting dish that's rich in protein and nutrients. It's an easy-to-make, wholesome meal perfect for any day of the week.

Servings: 4

Cook Time: 6-8 hours

Prepping Time: 15 minutes

Difficulty: Easy

Ingredients:

- ✓ 1 lb ground beef
- ✓ 1 egg
- ✓ 1/2 cup almond flour (optional, for binding)
- ✓ 4 cups beef broth
- ✓ 1 cup carrots, sliced
- ✓ 1 cup zucchini, chopped
- ✓ 1 onion, chopped
- ✓ 2 garlic cloves, minced
- ✓ 1 tsp thyme
- ✓ Salt and pepper to taste
- ✓ Fresh parsley for garnish

Step-by-Step Preparation:

1. In a bowl, mix the ground beef, egg, almond flour (optional), salt, and pepper to form meatballs.
2. Brown the meatballs in a skillet, then transfer to the slow cooker.
3. Add beef broth, sliced carrots, chopped zucchini, onion, garlic, thyme, salt, and pepper.
4. Set the slow cooker to low and cook for 6-8 hours until the vegetables are tender and the meatballs are fully cooked.
5. Serve hot, garnished with fresh parsley.

Nutritional Facts: (Per serving):

- ❖ Calories: 350
- ❖ Protein: 30g
- ❖ Fat: 18g
- ❖ Carbohydrates: 10g
- ❖ Fiber: 3g

This Meatball Soup with Vegetables is a nourishing, easy-to-prepare slow-cooker meal that fits perfectly into the Carnivore Diet. The tender meatballs and flavorful vegetables make it a satisfying and balanced dish that's perfect for family dinners or meal prep.

Recipe 50: German Pea Stew Erbsensuppe With Bacon

This German Pea Stew (Erbsensuppe) is a rich, hearty meal that fits perfectly into the Carnivore Diet. Slow-cooked with bacon, pork, carrots, and potatoes, this dish offers a flavorful combination of textures and savory spices. Infused with thyme, it's the perfect comfort food for any time of year.

Servings: 4

Prepping Time: 15 minutes

Cook Time: 6-8 hours

Difficulty: Easy

Ingredients:

- ✓ 1 lb pork shoulder, diced
- ✓ 6 slices of bacon, chopped
- ✓ 1 cup dried split peas
- ✓ 3 carrots, chopped
- ✓ 3 potatoes, chopped
- ✓ 1 onion, chopped
- ✓ 4 cups chicken broth
- ✓ 2 garlic cloves, minced
- ✓ 1 tsp thyme
- ✓ Salt and pepper to taste
- ✓ Fresh parsley for garnish

Step-by-Step Preparation:

1. Brown the bacon in a skillet, then transfer to the slow cooker.
2. Add diced pork, split peas, chopped carrots, potatoes, onion, garlic, thyme, salt, and pepper.
3. Pour the chicken broth over the ingredients.
4. Set the slow cooker to low and cook for 6-8 hours until the peas and meat are tender.
5. Stir and adjust seasoning if necessary.
6. Serve hot, garnished with fresh parsley.

Nutritional Facts: (Per serving):

- ❖ Calories: 400
- ❖ Protein: 30g
- ❖ Fat: 20g
- ❖ Carbohydrates: 25g
- ❖ Fiber: 5g

This German Pea Stew (Erbsensuppe) is a delicious, protein-packed slow-cooker meal, perfect for the Carnivore Diet. The combination of pork, bacon, and split peas creates a satisfying and hearty stew, ideal for warming up on cold days and bringing a taste of Germany to your kitchen.

Conclusion

As you reach the end of Delicious Carnivore Slow Cooker Recipes for Tender Meals, I hope this collection of hearty, flavor-packed dishes has inspired you to fully embrace the simplicity and satisfaction of slow cooking. Whether you're following the carnivore diet or simply looking for new ways to enjoy delicious, protein-rich meals, these recipes have been designed with care and attention to every detail.

This book is packed with 50 authentic, original recipes, divided into five delicious chapters:

✓ **Meat**

✓ **Chicken**

✓ **Fish**

✓ **Seafood**

✓ **Soup**

Each chapter offers 10 carefully selected recipes, from succulent meats to comforting soups, all cooked to perfection in your slow cooker. With colorful photos accompanying each dish, you'll have the confidence and inspiration to try every recipe and explore new flavors.

One of the key highlights of this cookbook is its accessibility. Every recipe has been crafted with easy-to-follow instructions, ensuring success whether you're a seasoned cook or a beginner. From the perfect tests for consistency to the vibrant flavors that burst with each bite, these recipes are sure to satisfy every palate.

Additionally, this book is printed in standard color, enhancing the visual appeal and providing a more enjoyable cooking experience. The stunning photography captures the beauty of each dish, helping you visualize the final result and guiding you through the cooking process.

As you continue on your culinary journey, I hope you find joy in preparing these meals, knowing that each recipe has been tested to ensure perfect results every time. From mouthwatering meats to nutrient-rich soups, this book is your guide to delicious, wholesome cooking.

Thank you for choosing Delicious Carnivore Slow Cooker Recipes for Tender Meals. May it serve as a lasting resource for you, bringing both nourishment and flavor to your table. Happy cooking!

Made in the USA
Las Vegas, NV
09 December 2024

13658305R00059